SHARKS

Photo-Fact Collection

Scientific Consultant
Diane Kelly
Ph. D., Zoology

Copyright © 2012 Kidsbooks, LLC
3535 West Peterson Avenue
Chicago, IL 60659

Printed in China
011201001SZ

Visit us at www.kidsbooks.com®

Hammerhead shark

CONTENTS

Shark!

Terrifying, magnificent, mysterious—sharks are masters of the sea. They are real survivors: in some form or another, they've been around for over 400 million years. Even before dinosaurs roamed the land, sharks ruled the oceans.

Tooth Tale

Scientists have found the teeth of a creature they call the Megalodon, a relative of the great white shark. It lived about 12,000 years ago, and it was huge. Its teeth were six inches long—more than twice the size of a great white's teeth.

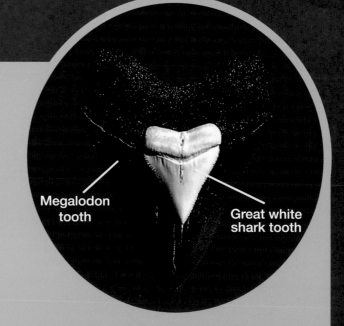

Megalodon tooth

Great white shark tooth

Bull shark

Blue shark

World Travelers

Sharks live all over the ocean, ranging from cold to tropical waters. Some live in shallow waters, while others live in the deep and on the ocean floor. Some, like the blue shark, travel thousands of miles. And some species, the bull shark in particular, can even swim from saltwater into freshwater.

Great white shark

Lemon shark

Meat Eaters

Almost all sharks are carnivores. They eat other fish, even other sharks, and sea mammals like dolphins and seals. The lemon shark often hunts for crabs and squid by using its yellow color to blend in with the sandy sea bottom.

Family Matters

There are more than 780 species of sharks, and they are very different from one another. Sharks belong to the group of fish known scientifically as elasmobranchs. Some are large, but most are fairly small. Only 39 species are over 10 feet long. The largest is the 60-foot whale shark, and the smallest is the 6-inch spined pygmy shark. One of the most easily identifiable sharks is the hammerhead shark—aptly named for its wide, mallet-shaped head.

Old Timer

Bullhead sharks are part of the oldest group of living sharks. Fossils of these sharks have been found in rocks 200 million years old. There are nine living species of bullhead shark, including the Port Jackson shark.

SPOOKY

It may be the strangest-looking shark of all. But because it lives in deep water, it's almost never seen! Until found off the coast of Japan in 1898, the goblin shark was believed to be extinct for 100 million years.

In the Tank

Some sharks are so gentle, they can be kept in aquariums. The zebra shark, also known as the leopard shark, is very gentle. It is spotted like a leopard, and its tail is half its length.

Push Up

A shark's tail is uneven. It is longer on the top than it is on the bottom. Scientists think this design produces lift. As the shark beats its tail to move forward, its body also gets pushed upward in the water.

Blacktip reef shark

Caribbean reef shark

Sink or Swim

Most bony fish have a swim bladder that fills with air to keep them afloat when they are not swimming. A shark doesn't. It has to keep swimming to keep from sinking. But the shark has at least one flotation device—a big, oil-filled liver, which helps keep the shark afloat.

Pectoral fin

Oceanic whitetip shark

Hands Off

The skin of most fish has scales, but shark scales are different. Called "denticles," shark scales are constructed like very hard, sharp teeth. Scales feel smooth when rubbed one way but can tear skin if rubbed the other way.

Built to Last

A shark glides through the sea. Its pectoral fins are stiff and are used for going up and down. The caudal fin is moved from side to side to propel the shark forward. Although some sharks can go fast enough to leap out of the water, sharks aren't built to swim fast all the time. Sharks are built to cruise slowly for long distances.

Dorsal fin

Gills Galore

Most fish use gills to breathe. Water passes into their mouth and out over the gills, which absorb oxygen from the water into the fish's bloodstream. Unlike most fish, which only have a single gill covering, sharks have five to seven gill slits.

Caudal fin

Super Sharp Senses

A shark can hear, smell, and feel everything in the water at great distances. Its super sharp senses make the shark an excellent hunter. A school of fish may be passing through, or a fish may be hurt. The shark knows the difference and it reacts quickly, zooming toward its prey with deadly accuracy.

Blacktip reef shark

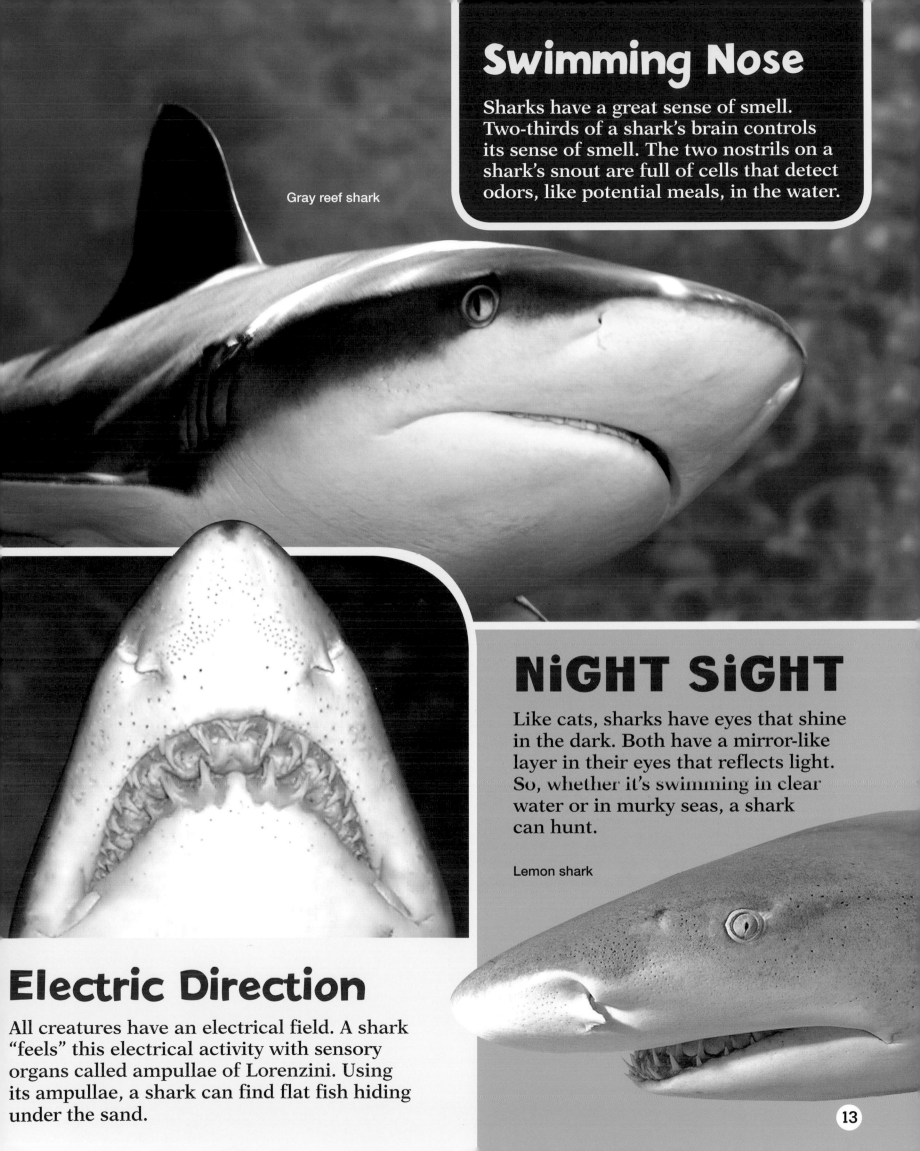

Swimming Nose

Sharks have a great sense of smell. Two-thirds of a shark's brain controls its sense of smell. The two nostrils on a shark's snout are full of cells that detect odors, like potential meals, in the water.

Gray reef shark

NiGHT SiGHT

Like cats, sharks have eyes that shine in the dark. Both have a mirror-like layer in their eyes that reflects light. So, whether it's swimming in clear water or in murky seas, a shark can hunt.

Lemon shark

Electric Direction

All creatures have an electrical field. A shark "feels" this electrical activity with sensory organs called ampullae of Lorenzini. Using its ampullae, a shark can find flat fish hiding under the sand.

A Bite to Eat

Born with a mouth full of teeth, sharks bite, crunch, and swallow their meals. Normally, sharks dine alone. But every now and then they have a vicious party, sometimes called a feeding frenzy. One feeding shark may attract others. Racing to the scene, they slash at the prey and bite wildly at anything that gets in their way—even each other. Then, it's over as quickly as it began.

Messy Eater

Sharks bite, but they do not chew. They swallow things whole or in big pieces. Some use their teeth like a fork and knife—they have pointed teeth in the lower jaw to puncture prey, and serrated teeth in the top to saw away at meat.

Great white shark

CRUNCH!

When a shark bites, both its upper and lower jaws move. It strikes with its lower jaw first, then the upper, and flings its head from side to side to tear loose a piece of meat.

Dental Plan

Sharks have a lifetime supply of teeth, with rows and rows set in soft tissue. An adult probably goes through 7 to 12 sets in one year. Each time a tooth is lost by biting or through aging, a new tooth moves forward and takes its place. Some sharks, like the cookiecutter, swallow whole sets of teeth during one meal!

Cannibal Baby

A female sand tiger shark carries eggs that hatch inside its body. It produces many eggs, but the first to hatch is sometimes the only one born. This baby may eat its underdeveloped brothers and sisters. When it's born, the baby is about one-third the size of its mother.

THAT'S AN EGG?

Shark eggs are not "egg-shaped" like chicken eggs. They are tough, leathery, and rectangular, or shaped like spirals and screws. As the baby shark develops inside this egg case, it feeds on the yolk part like chickens do. In 8 to 14 months, a shark is fully developed, and even has teeth!

Port Jackson shark egg

Special Delivery

There are three different ways that sharks can begin life. One way is to hatch from eggs outside their mother's body, the way chickens do. Alternatively, they can hatch from eggs inside their mother before they are born. Or, like people, their mother can give birth to them. Sharks have from 1 to 100 babies at a time, depending on the way they reproduce. Species that give birth to fully-developed sharks have fewer babies at a time than sharks that lay eggs outside their bodies.

Dogfish shark egg

Tough Pups

A baby shark is called a pup, but it doesn't lead a dog's life. Its mother doesn't feed it or give it hunting lessons. To survive, many young sharks go close to shore to grow up on their own. There are small fish to feed on there and no large sharks around.

Spotted cat shark

Types of Sharks

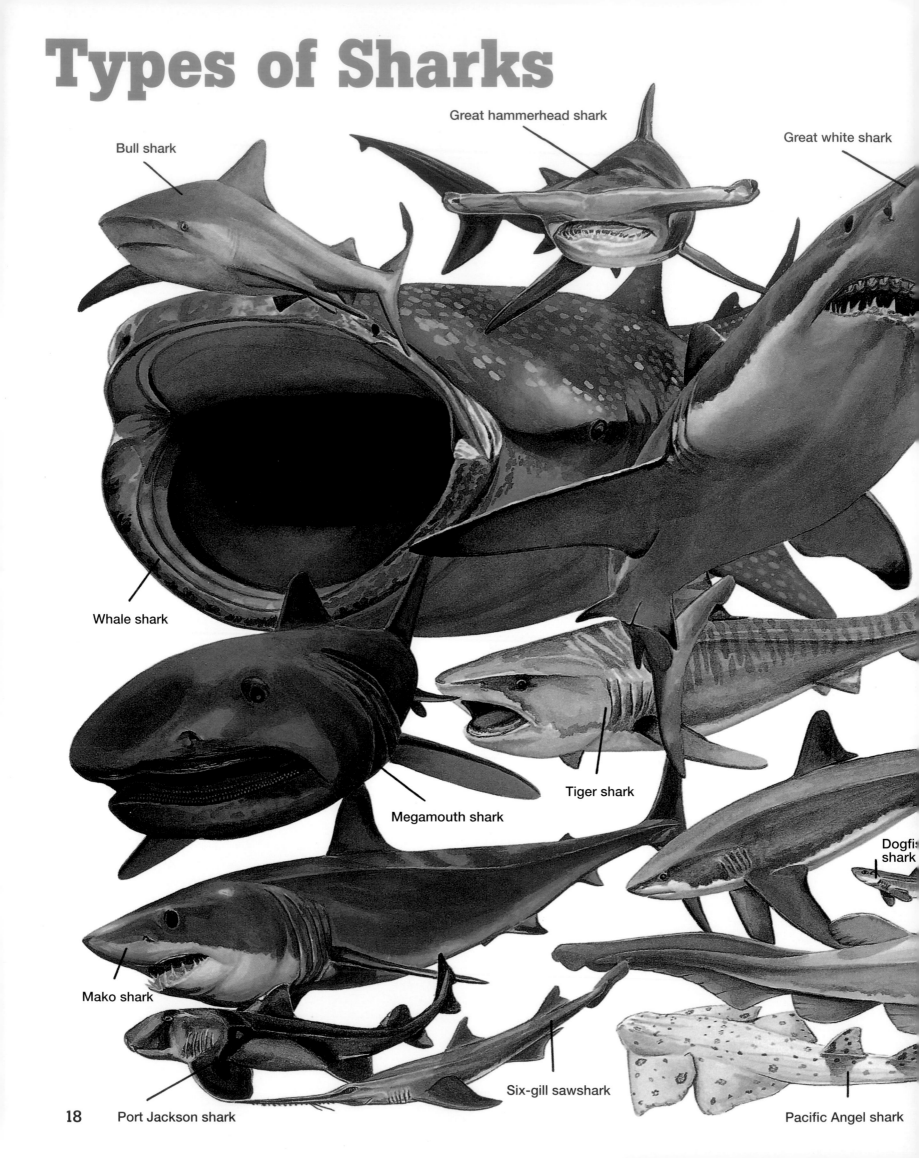

Bull shark

Great hammerhead shark

Great white shark

Whale shark

Megamouth shark

Tiger shark

Dogfish shark

Mako shark

Port Jackson shark

Six-gill sawshark

Pacific Angel shark

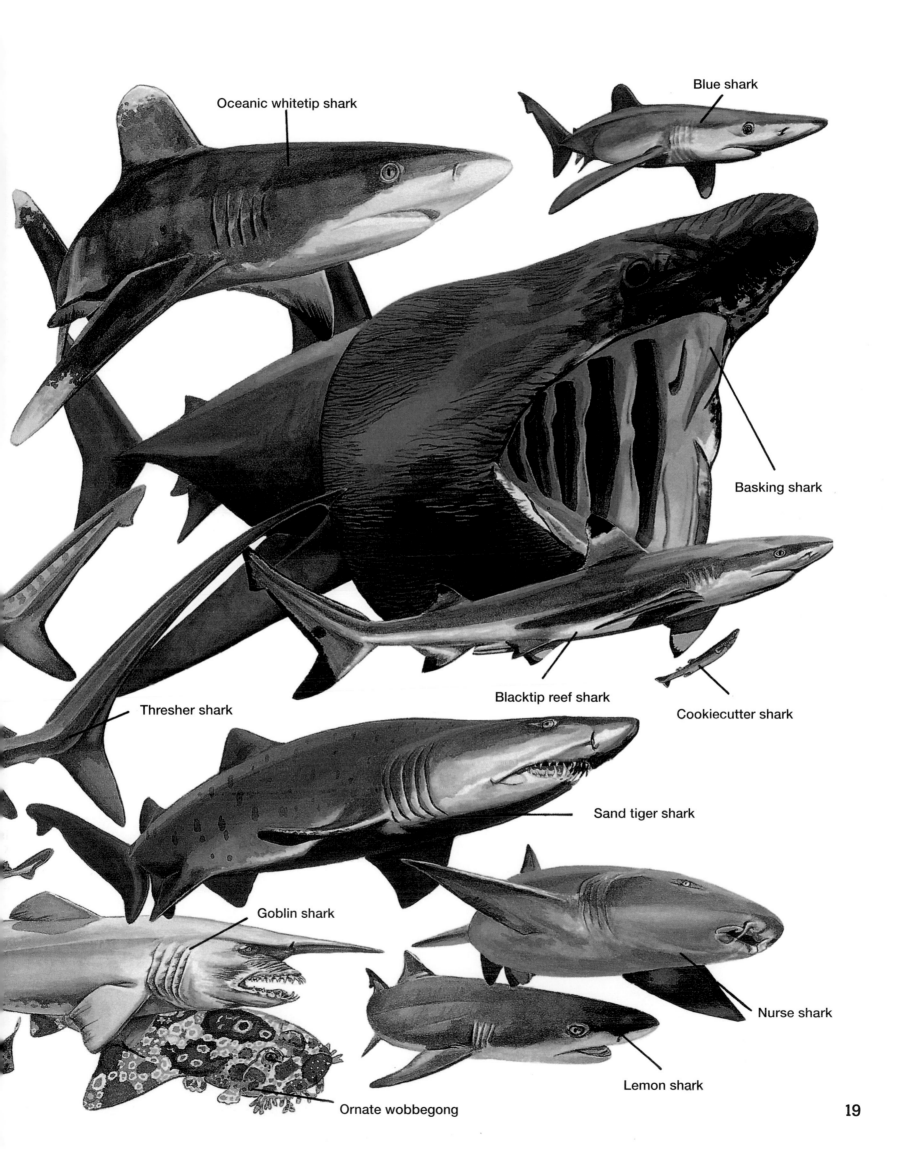

Oceanic whitetip shark

Blue shark

Basking shark

Thresher shark

Blacktip reef shark

Cookiecutter shark

Sand tiger shark

Goblin shark

Nurse shark

Lemon shark

Ornate wobbegong

19

Danger!

Worldwide, sharks attack fewer than 100 people in an average year, and half of these are by tiger sharks, bull sharks, and the great white. Attacks usually occur where there are a lot of people, in fairly warm, waist-deep water. It's possible that all the vibrations in the water resemble those of a wounded fish—a shark's favorite meal.

Great white shark

Speedy Swimmer

The mako is powerful and thought to be dangerous. It is the fastest shark of all, clocked at 43 miles per hour. It is known to leap out of water and sometimes onto boats!

Brutal Bull

The bull shark doesn't look as frightening as the great white, but it is in some ways more dangerous, especially in the tropics. Listed as the third most dangerous man-eater, the bull shark swims in places that people do—in saltwater and fresh water.

Tiger of the Sea

The tiger shark is second only to the great white in terms of the number of people it attacks. There is very little in the sea that the tiger shark doesn't eat. Some have been found with weird objects in their bellies, such as boat cushions, unopened cans of salmon, an alarm clock, tar paper, and a keg of nails!

21

Huge & Harmless

Sharks are not always fierce and aggressive. Some sharks are harmless. And, strangely enough, the most harmless sharks are huge. These two characteristics, which do not seem to go together, belong to the basking shark, whale shark, and megamouth shark. They are the gentle giants of the shark family. The whale shark is the largest fish in the world, growing up to about 40 feet long.

Big Surprise

In 1976, a navy ship off the coast of Hawaii accidentally hauled in a type of shark that had never before been discovered. It weighed over 6,000 pounds. Scientists gave it a name to fit its face: megamouth. It was another harmless, giant shark.

Mini-Food

These big sharks eat plankton. Copepods—barely visible shrimplike creatures—are a large part of plankton. Scientists figure that sharks eat about one percent of their body's weight each day. For an 8,000 pound basking shark, that's a lot of plankton—80 pounds!

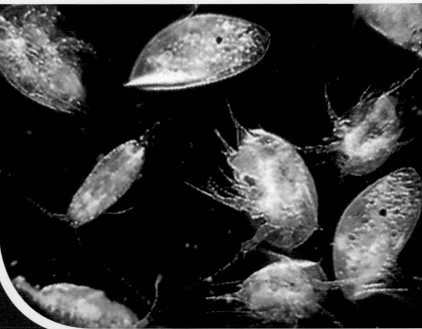

SUNBATHERS

A basking shark can usually grow to be 30 feet long and 8,000 pounds. This fish is a mammoth sunbather. Its name comes from its habit of lying motionless in surface waters with its back above the surface and its nose and fins sticking out—as if it were "basking" in the sun.

Manta rays

Bluespotted ribbontail ray

Risky Ray

Lurking in coastal waters around the world are more than 100 kinds of stingrays. Some grow very large, weighing well over 600 pounds. The stingray has a poisonous dagger, or spine, on its tail, and it lies on the ocean floor in shallow waters. If a swimmer steps on it, the result may be a sting or much worse—paralysis!

Egg Purse

Skates are bottom-dwelling rays that glide along the ocean floor with rippling fins. Their egg cases look like little black rectangles with strings. Long ago, people who found them thought mermaids left them. Even today, the skate's egg cases are called "mermaid's purses."

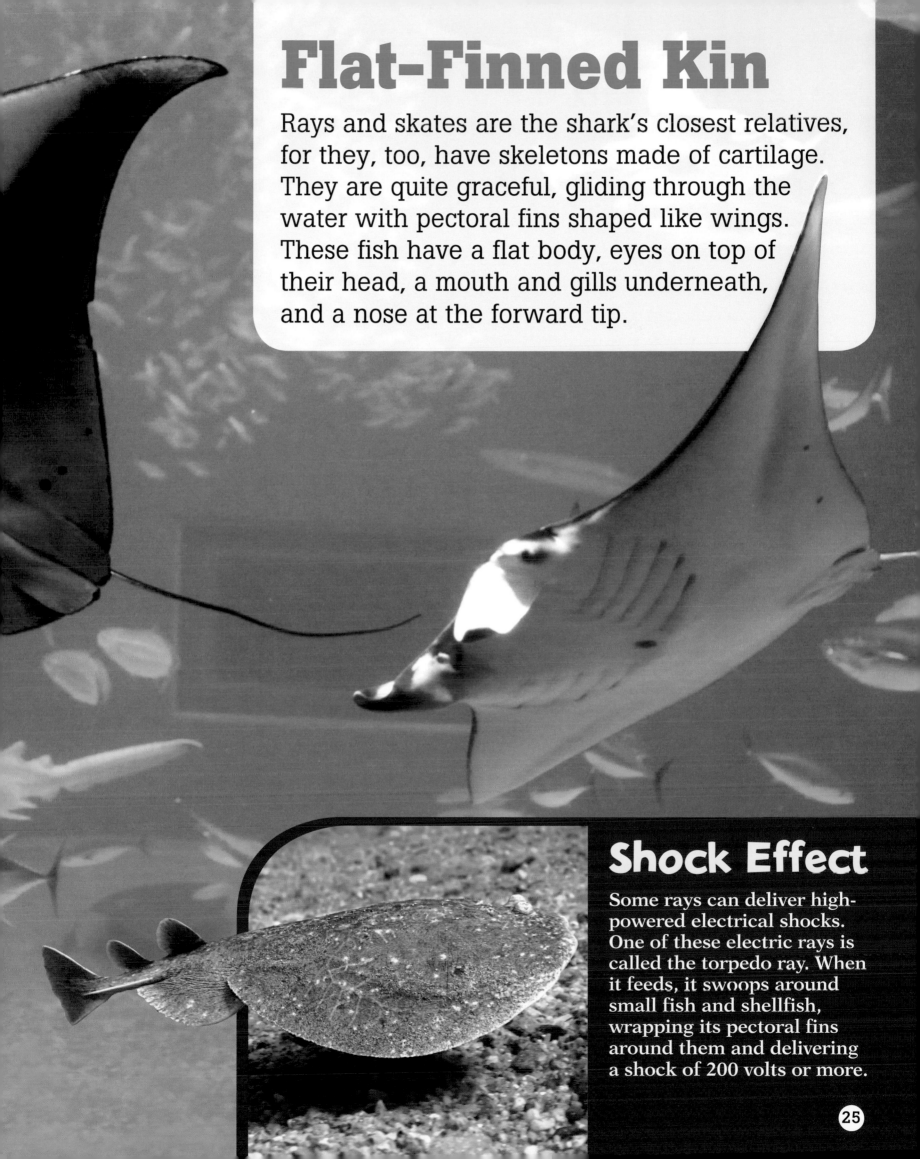

Flat-Finned Kin

Rays and skates are the shark's closest relatives, for they, too, have skeletons made of cartilage. They are quite graceful, gliding through the water with pectoral fins shaped like wings. These fish have a flat body, eyes on top of their head, a mouth and gills underneath, and a nose at the forward tip.

Shock Effect

Some rays can deliver high-powered electrical shocks. One of these electric rays is called the torpedo ray. When it feeds, it swoops around small fish and shellfish, wrapping its pectoral fins around them and delivering a shock of 200 volts or more.

The Deep

What's more mysterious than the bottom of the deep blue sea? The sharks that live there! There are many different types of bottom-dwelling sharks, and a few of them are really strange looking. Some eat mussels, clams, and snails. Others prey on the swimming creatures that share their home. Nurse sharks, a type of slow-moving bottom-dweller, use their strong jaws to crush and eat shellfish and coral, as well as fish, shrimp, and squid.

Devilish Angel

Angel sharks act more like devils. Although the angel lounges motionless on the bottom, it has a swift and deadly bite, with sharp, dagger-like teeth to impale fish and crustaceans. Fisherman who have tangled with it call it the "sand devil."

Pacific angel shark

Sawtooth

The sawshark has teeth on the outside of its mouth. It has a long, flat, blade-like snout with teeth on either side, like a saw. Unborn sawsharks have soft teeth that are folded back until birth, when contact with salt water hardens them. This protects the mother carrying the baby shark inside her body

Killer Carpet

The carpet shark has a special hunting plan: camouflage, so it can sneak up on unsuspecting prey! Carpet sharks have markings that blend in with the sand, and a head that can look like a mop of weeds.

Tasselled wobbegong

Sharks & People

The shark is often used as a symbol for things that are frightening or dangerous. However, scientists who study sharks have learned that sharks are not simply killing machines. In fact, people are more dangerous to sharks than sharks are to people. We hunt them, pollute their water, and cause them injury, sometimes depleting whole populations.

Blacktip reef shark

Skin Deep

People have hunted sharks and rays for their skin for centuries. Sharkskin is 100% stronger than cowhide. It's used like any other leather to make products such as shoes, belts, and purses.

Mako shark

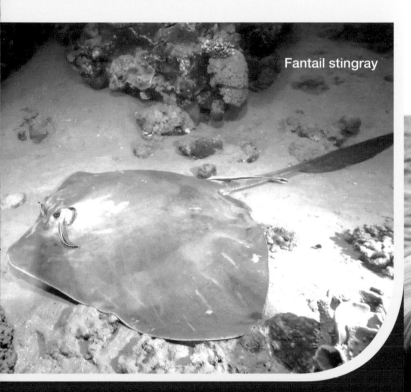

Fantail stingray

End of the Line?

As more and more people catch sharks for food, the number of sharks is shrinking quickly. Since the 1980s, some shark populations have shrunk more than 80%. More than 50 shark species arc now threatened or endangered, including the oceanic whitetip, the broadfin, and the scalloped hammerhead shark.

Scalloped hammerhead shark

Totally Toxic

Sharks are at the top of the ocean food chain so pollution collects in their bodies. That can make shark meat dangerous for people to eat. One recent study found mako shark meat had mercury levels six times higher than safe levels.

GLOSSARY

Aggressive: Ready to confront or attack.

Ampullae of Lorenzini: Sensory cells that help sharks detect electrical activity from the nerves and muscles of the fish they hunt.

Camouflage: The way an animal disguises and protects itself by blending with its surroundings.

Carnivore: An animal that eats the flesh of other animals.

Cartilage: Soft, flexible material that joins one bone to another. Human ears and noses are made up of cartilage, as are the skeletons of sharks and rays.

Caudal fin: Fin that helps a shark or other fish move forward; also known as a tail fin.

Copepods: Small shrimplike creatures that are a large part of plankton eaten by large sharks.

Crustaceans: Joint-legged animals with a hard outer covering; includes lobsters and crabs.

Denticles: Hard, toothlike scales on a shark.

Depletion: Reduced in numbers.

Egg case: Tough outer covering of a shark egg, often shaped like spirals, screws, or rectangles. Each egg case holds one egg.

Elasmobranchs: The family of fish to which sharks and rays belong.

Endangered: An animal that is in danger of going extinct.

Extinct: A species without any living members.

Feeding frenzy: An excited pursuit of food by a group of sharks.

Flotation device: Something that floats in or on the surface of a fluid. A shark uses its oil-filled liver to float.

Fossil: Any evidence of an ancient living thing that has been naturally preserved.

Gills: Breathing organs of fish and other water animals. Most fish have one pair of gill slits, but sharks have five to seven pairs.

Megalodon: Ancestor of the great white shark that lived about 12,000 years ago.

Murky: Not clear, hard to see through.

Paralysis: Complete or partial loss of function, especially when involving motion or sensation in a part of the body. Some stingrays cause paralysis to humans.

Pectoral fin: Fin on each side of a fish's chest used for balance.

Plankton: Tiny animals and plants living in the sea that are the basic food for larger sea animals, such as whales and whale sharks.

Prey: An animal that is hunted by other animals.

Propel: To push forward or onward.

Pup: Baby shark.

Ray: A type of flat, broad fish, including stingrays and skates, that usually lives on the sea bottom. These creatures have eyes on the upper surface of their bodies, a long, narrow tail, and a skeleton made of cartilage.

School: A group of fish that swim together, often for protection from predators.

Serrated: Notched at the edge, like the blades of saws or steak knives. A shark's teeth are serrated.

Slit: A long narrow strip. Sharks have five to seven gill slits on their sides.

Snout: A long nose that projects from the head, or a face or head that is long and narrow.

Swim bladder: Most bony fish have this organ that fills with air to keep them afloat. Sharks do not have one.

Vibrations: Quivering or trembling motions that can be heard or felt.